I0822222
To:
From:
Date:

with Love
INSPIRATIONAL GIFTS